DECODING SILENCE

Reading Body Language to Understand Emotion and Predict Actions

by
Justine Hart

Dear Esteemed Reader,

Thank you immensely for choosing this book to join your collection. We imagine that you've already embarked on an exploration of ideas within these pages, and we couldn't be happier about it!

Now, if you find yourself chuckling, pondering, or even debating with the words in front of you, we'd absolutely love to hear about it. If you can spare a few moments to pen down your thoughts in a review, we would be as delighted as a dictionary on a spelling bee!

An Amazon review would be excellent - but hey, we're far from picky. Whether it's a scribble on the back of a grocery list, a tweet, or even a message in a bottle (though that might take a while to reach us), your feedback is gold.

Writing a review might not be as fun as a spontaneous dance-off, but we promise it'll bring grins to our faces, warmth to our hearts, and incredibly valuable insights to future readers.

With Gratitude,

Bo Bennett, PhD
Publisher
Archieboy Holdings, LLC.

Table of Contents

Introduction to Body Language and Emotion

Welcome! You've embarked on a fascinating journey into the realm of body language and emotion, a subject rich in complexity and intertwined with our everyday interactions. This journey is for those who are eager to better understand the unspoken cues that color our communications and have a decisive impact on our interactions. Whether it's a casual chat with a friend or a tense business negotiation, body language is vital as it bridges the gap between words spoken and the intentions behind them.

We've all heard the saying "Actions speak louder than words", right? Well, in this context, it couldn't be more accurate. The science of body language extends way beyond simple hand movements or facial expressions. It delves deep into the world of non-verbal signals, offering a fresh perspective on how we translate the silent messages people send. From the subtle nuances of facial expressions to the profound impact of postures, you'll get a grasp on what it means to communicate beyond words. And, it's not just about understanding others, but also about becoming aware of your own body language and the powerful message it sends out.

We're going to delve deeper into understanding how body language intertwines with human emotions, how the underlying science aids in decoding these silent signals, and how it is used practically in everyday interactions. We'll explore how body language can telegraph happiness, sadness, anger, fear, surprise, and disgust, romping through the commonly held misconceptions to find the truth. With every page you turn, get ready to unlock new insights and arm yourself with knowledge that's going to open a whole new world of communication. So here's your guide to becoming a pro at reading, understanding, and using body language to your advantage. Let's get started!

Understanding the Basics

So, where do you start to peel back the hidden layers of a conversation? It's simple, we start with the basics of body language and emotion. Body language, plainly put, is a form of non-verbal communication composed of postures, gestures, facial expressions, and eye movements. It is how people express their emotions, thoughts, and feelings without saying a word.

The key to reading body language is understanding that our bodies communicate just as much, if not more, than our words. Think about it, you may say one thing, but your body might be screaming something entirely different. This discrepancy usually gives away what we are really thinking or feeling.

Let's consider a simple example: You're having a conversation with a friend who is beaming a big smile and saying everything's great, but their shoulders are slumped and their gaze is lowered. Even if you can't put a finger on the specifics, instinctually, something feels 'off'. These inconsistencies often help us sense a person's true message.

Next, we need to realize that emotions play a massive role in body language. Emotions are transient, complex states of feeling that result in physical and psychological changes which influence thought and behavior. When we're scared, happy or stressed, it all manifests physically in some way.

Gesticulating while talking, constant shuffling of feet, darting eyes, or even a consistent smile are all different ways emotions come to the surface in non-verbal form. Understanding emotions helps us to read and interpret these signals more effectively. We actually do this all the time subconsciously, but with some practice, we could improve our conscious recognition of these cues.

Another thing that we can't ignore in this puzzle is the cultural context. Gestures or postures that might be completely normal in one society could be offensive or misunderstood in another. For instance, a thumbs up is generally considered positive in the US, but in some Middle Eastern cultures, it could be misconstrued as a rude gesture.

Then, of course, we have our own personal quirks and habits. Each one of us has a unique body language vocabulary that is so deeply ingrained that we're generally not aware of it. Though some aspects of body language are universally understood, the full message of a person's body language can often be appreciated only when we get to know them better.

Finally, let's talk about intuition. Sometimes, you might just 'feel' that someone is unhappy or hiding something. This 'gut feeling' is often based on our fast, intuitive processing of body language cues. While intuition shouldn't be the sole basis of your judgments, it can provide helpful pointers in understanding the basics of body language and emotion.

To sum up, body language isn't just about 'reading' people, it's equally about being more aware and mindful of our own non-verbal cues. This will not only enhance our interactions with others but also help us stay in touch with our own emotional state.

In a way, body language is like an additional language, one that is spoken by our bodies, perceived by our eyes, and understood by our brains. Mastering this language can open new avenues for us in terms of daily communication, better understanding of self and others, and enriching our emotional expressiveness.

Understanding the basics of body language and emotion isn't as intimidating as you might think, and it doesn't require a degree in psychology. It just needs a keen eye, a mindful approach and the willingness to learn and adapt. Decomposing the complexities and cracking the code of body language can be thrilling, intuitive, and indeed quite enlightening!

The power of body language and emotions can't be overstated. It can indeed act as a mirror to the soul, reflecting our deepest thoughts, feelings, and intentions. So let's embark on this fascinating journey and discover how unspoken words can often speak the loudest.

Now that we've gone over the basics of body language and emotion, imagine the edge you could have in your next interaction. Understanding what is not said gives us an insight that is just as important as what is being verbally articulated. Whether you're looking to advance in your career or improve your relationships, learning to read body language is an invaluable skill in the human experience. Let's now dive into the power of non-verbal communication!

Chapter 1:
Power of Non-Verbal Communication

Continuing from our introduction of body language fundamentals, we dive headfirst into the captivating world of non-verbal communication, an often overlooked arena that holds the key to understanding the unspoken emotions of the people around us. Throughout our daily lives, we unknowingly send and receive a plethora of messages without uttering a single word. These non-verbal cues primarily manifest as subtle changes in facial expressions, shifts in postures, and varied gestures. Often overshadowed by the spoken word, the potency of these silent dialogues cannot be understated. By mastering non-verbal communication, the veil concealing the unexpressed thoughts and sentiments of others can easily be lifted, revealing a wealth of information that was hiding in plain view. This art, if harnessed correctly, can empower you to predict, understand, and respond to underlying emotions that are silently echoed throughout a conversation, providing you a step ahead in any interaction. Getting a firm grasp of these subtleties is akin to unlocking a superpower that equips you with a unique ability to connect with others on a deeper, more intimate level. The following sections will delve into exploring the nuances of facial expressions and interpreting postures and gestures, helping you to not only observe but also comprehend these silent yet powerful exchanges.

Grasping the Subtleties

Body language is more than the broad brushstrokes of communication. It thrives in the subtle cues that often go unnoticed during our day-to-day interactions. As we dive deeper into the realm of non-verbal communication, it's critical to understand these nuanced aspects that enrich our ability to connect with others.

Every facet of our behavior - a tilt of the head, the pacing of our speech, or even the grip of our handshake - has the potential to convey volumes of information. This hidden reservoir of communication can add layers of meaning to our conversations, aiding in creating more profound, more meaningful connections with those around us.

A major part of grasping these subtleties lies in becoming aware of your own body movements. As you observe your own behavior, you'll quickly realize how much you communicate non-verbally, often without conscious intent. This heightened awareness can then be turned outward, encouraging a more deliberate and attentive reading of others.

A gentle touch on the forearm, for instance, could signify empathy, mutual understanding, or even romantic interest, based on context. The ability to accurately interpret this action must be learned and honed over time, and is one of the numerous subtleties that constitute the larger picture of body language.

Beyond the conscious gestures, seemingly involuntary movements can also carry substantial cues. Consider, for example, the tendency to blink more when we're uncomfortable or lying. An increased blink rate is not something we typically control, yet it's a telltale signal to those attuned to the subtleties of non-verbal communication.

Another relatively overlooked aspect is the element of timing. It's not just what body language cue is being displayed, but also when it's expressed that matters. Abrupt changes in posture, for example, might be indicative of veiled tension or discomfort, while maintaining direct eye contact longer than the average span can be an assertion of dominance or confidence.

We also can't underestimate the role of cultural differences when assessing non-verbal cues. What may constitute a sign of respect in one culture, like avoiding eye contact, could be interpreted as a lack of confidence in another. Navigating these cultural nuances is another essential facet of effectively understanding non-verbal communication.

One of the challenging aspects in mastering non-verbal communication comes from the fact that cues may contradict each other or clash with verbal communication. You might encounter someone who's verbally consenting, yet their stiff posture, crossed arms, or fidgety hands suggest discomfort. These are 'mixed signals', suggesting a divergence between their thoughts and their words.

While attempting to unravel these nuances, remember that no single gesture or signal has a fixed meaning in isolation. Each must be evaluated in concert with others, taking into account the overall situation and context. Context is king in the universe of body language - it provides the necessary backdrop against which individual gestures acquire meaning.

For example, crossed arms could signify defensiveness, insecurity or vulnerability. However, in a cold room it might just mean the person is trying to stay warm! Understanding and considering the context helps prevent misinterpretation of these signals.

Moreover, don't think of this as an exact science, but rather as an art. Your intuition or 'gut feeling' can be a powerful tool for deciphering non-verbal cues. If something feels off, it's worth taking the time to explore why you feel that way. It might be that your subconscious has noticed a discrepancy in body language that hasn't yet surfaced to conscious thought.

At the end of the day, effective communication isn't about catching every single non-verbal cue. It's about becoming more conscious of the variety of ways people express themselves and validating these expressions with empathy and understanding.

Immersing yourself in the subtleties of non-verbal communication opens up a world of connectivity that many tend to overlook. So keep your eyes open, your intuition sharp, and you will uncover a different layer to every conversation, increasing depth in your interactions and fostering stronger, more genuine connections.

As we move forward, we'll delve deeper into specific components of non-verbal communication, beginning with facial expressions - a critical and rich source of information about what people are feeling and thinking.

Exploring Nuances of Facial Expressions – when we delve into the world of facial expressions, we realize its depth and complexity. Having the capability to comprehend and evaluate facial expressions is one of the ways we can push the envelope to understand others better.

One aspect of facial expressions is their universality. Regardless of cultural or geographical distinctions, certain facial expressions are recognized worldwide. Happiness, conveyed by a smile, sadness, signified by a downturned mouth or teary eyes, and anger, shown by a furrowed brow, are unmistakable regardless of where you are. Despite the uniqueness of every human being, our faces use a somewhat universal language to express fundamental emotions.

Then again, not all facial expressions are that straightforward. Certainly, wide smiles and furrowed brows are easy to interpret, but what about the subtler expressions? For instance, consider a lightened look in the eyes, a vertical furrow between the eyebrows, or even the relaxation of facial muscles. These nuances can express a myriad of feelings, from contemplation to discomfort, but their interpretation depends heavily on the context.

Interestingly, our faces are not just a canvas for our emotions, but also a portal into our minds. When someone is engaged in critical thinking or deep concentration, they may exhibit facial microexpressions. These are transient, often involuntary expressions that might escape notice unless you're specifically looking for them. They can be as subtle as a microscopic squint or a barely-there grimace, and are generally difficult to fake or control.

Understanding the concept of microexpressions, and how to read them, can aid you greatly in engaging with others. They offer clues about what a person might be truly feeling or thinking, despite what their words might express. For instance, a fleeting look of disgust or discomfort could indicate disagreement or disbelief, even if verbally they're agreeing with you. Conversely, a quick flash of a genuine smile, even during a seemingly serious conversation, can signify happiness or approval.

Delving deeper, it's also critical to pay attention to how and when these expressions occur. Timing and duration can say a lot about the sincerity of an expression. Genuine emotions tend to both appear and vanish in a relatively smooth manner, whereas controlled or manipulated feelings can change too abruptly or last too long to be authentic.

The position and movement of eyebrows is another nuance keenly detected by our brains. Raised eyebrows can express surprise or confusion, while a single raised eyebrow may indicate skepticism. Lowered eyebrows can signal concentration, but if the brow is furrowed, it might suggest anger or displeasure.

Moreover, remember that facial expressions must always be interpreted in a broader context, comprising other body language, speech, and situation. A smirk during a serious conversation might denote arrogance or dismissal, but the same gesture in a casual setting could be a signal of humor. Context is crucial in understanding the layered world of facial expressions.

In conclusion, exploring the nuances of facial expressions is more than just understanding and reading into the major expressions of happiness, sadness, anger, etc. It's about paying attention to the subtleties, the minute details that could reveal information not ordinarily perceived. Mastering this art would definitely put you a step ahead in your interactions and communications.

Interpreting Postures and Gestures is essential to effectively understanding body language and accurately interpreting the unspoken sentiments of others. Postures and gestures provide a wealth of information that can often disclose a person's real feelings and intentions, even when they are speaking words to the contrary. You'd be amazed at what you can learn from the way someone positions their body or moves their hands during a conversation. Let's unravel this.

When observing posture, consider the entire body and its orientation. A forward leaning posture, for example, typically indicates interest and engagement, while a backward lean can imply discomfort or disinterest. Straight posture demonstrates self-assurance and confidence, while slouching may signal lack of engagement, uncertainty, or exhaustion.

Beyond posture, one's gestures can reveal a lot. Hand gestures can be incredibly expressive, often amplifying or clarifying verbal communication. For instance, if someone keeps their hands hidden, it might suggest that they are holding back or concealing something. On the other hand, active and visible hand gestures can denote openness and honesty.

Thumbs play a striking role within hand gestures. Thumbs up can be a sign of approval or victory, while seeing the back of someone's hand accompanied by an extended thumb might signal a 'thumbs down' or disapproval. The thumb might also be hidden when an individual feels insecure or unsure.

Arm gestures, too, are loaded with meaning. Crossed arms, for example, can indicate self-protection, discomfort, or defensiveness. Exposed palms, conversely, generally suggest honesty and acceptance. Arm gestures often mirror our inner fears or comforts and can be used to create or reduce space between us and others.

We also use our feet and legs to express ourselves. The direction in which our feet point often shows where our interest lies. If someone's feet are pointed toward you during a conversation, it usually means they're engaged. If their feet point toward the door, however, they probably want to leave.

Overall, our bodies speak volumes in the nuances of posture and gesture. But remember, context matters. Interpreting these signals in relation to the surrounding environment and the ongoing conversation is key as body language is not a one-size-fits-all scenario.

The incorporation of a knowledge of postures and gestures has the potential to dramatically enhance interpersonal communication, yielding a richer depth of understanding. As natural as it can be to digest spoken words, tuning into the language of postures and gestures makes for an even more complete conversation.

However, it's important to remember that while these insights can be arousively revealing, they are not foolproof. No single gesture or posture reveals the whole picture. Rather, each contributes a piece to a larger, more complex puzzle that can only truly be understood when considering all the pieces together. It can be quite amazing to experience those 'aha' moments and the heightened sense of understanding that comes with interpreting postures and gestures correctly.

Take time to hone your skills in observing and interpreting postures and gestures, and you'll find yourself becoming more adept at connecting and communicating effectively with others. It's an art, an investment in your personal and professional life you won't regret.

Chapter 2:
The Science of Body Language

Shifting from a social perspective to a scientific one, exploring the realm of body language yields insights that are nothing short of astounding. As we delve into the science of body language, fully understanding biological signals is paramount. We'll start by examining the neurological basis of our bodily gestures and expressions, which can reveal a stunning amount more than spoken words. You see, our brain is constantly firing cues for our body to behave in certain ways based on our thoughts or the situation around us. Moving along, hormones - the body's invisible puppeteers - play a significant role in orchestrating our behavioral patterns, and understanding their impact can be a game-changer in our voyage to decipher body language. Lastly, we'll peek into the enigmatic discipline of psychophysiology, exploring how psychological phenomena manifest physically. This voyage through biology, neuroscience, and psychology promises to equip us with the skills to decode body language at an even fundamentally deeper level.

Decoding Biological Signals

As we delve into the fascinating world of body language, it's paramount to understand the biological signals that underpin our non-verbal communication. Just like a skilled linguist deciphers an alien dialect, we'll peel back the onion layers to reveal the intricate world of body language and its deep roots in our biology.

So, what are these biological signals, and why should we care? Well, think of them as your body's way of communicating even when your mouth is locked in a poker face. They give away important clues, often subconsciously, about what you're feeling, thinking, or planning. This communication can be as nuanced as a quick flick of the wrist or as blatant as a heavy sigh.

One of the first indicators is body temperature. It might come as a surprise, but our bodily processes can can trigger noticeable changes in body heat. When feeling stress or anxiety, our bodies heat up as survival mechanism. This change manifests as sweaty palms or a flushed face. If you notice these cues in a conversation, you might be pushing too hard or dealing with someone who isn't comfortable.

Pupil dilation is another biological signal rooted in our primal instincts. Increased adrenaline levels, often associated with either attraction or threat, cause our pupils to dilate. Body language experts often gauge their partner's interest or possible threat levels by observing the subtly changing patterns of their pupils.

Posture serves as another primary source of communication. Have you ever noticed how someone who's upset or defensive will often stand with arms folded and shoulders hunched? It's not a coincidence. This stance acts as a physical barrier, reflecting a closed and defensive mindset. The reverse, a relaxed open posture, suggests receptiveness and openness to communication.

The way we move, our locomotion, also plays a vital role in decoding biological signals. Somebody who is eager, for instance, walks briskly with broader steps, while a person with a sluggish walk might be displaying signs of exhaustion, disinterest, or even depression.

Facial expressions are arguably among the most informative biological signals. A fake smile stops at the lips, while a genuine one lights up the entire face. Raised eyebrows can denote surprise or skepticism, while a furrowed brow might indicate concentration or confusion.

Physical touch, although sometimes overlooked, is another integral part of biological signaling. A firm handshake usually denotes confidence, a pat on the back shows support, while a soft touch on the arm can show genuine interest in a person or their conversation.

Respiratory rates shouldn't be underestimated. Nervous people often have quick, shallow breaths, while those who are relaxed or in control take deeper, slower breaths. If you notice an individual's breathing becoming increasingly rapid during a conversation, it could indicate rising stress or discomfort levels.

Even intricacies such as skin color changes can signal emotional shifts. For instance, blushing often occurs when we're embarrassed, while going pale can indicate fear or shock.

It's important to emphasize that no single biological signal can give us a complete reading of what an individual is undergoing or intending. Only by observing a combination of these signals and considering the context, can we arrive at an accurate interpretation.

Keep in mind that individual differences also play a significant role in biological signaling. What comes naturally to one person may not manifest identically in another. Yet, with the right understanding and a keen eye for these signals, anyone can enhance their ability to read others beyond what they verbalize.

With these biological signals in mind, let's dig deeper into the science of body language by learning about the neurological basis, the role of hormones, and delving into the realm of psychophysiology. Are you ready? Let's dive deeper and gorge ourselves on the feast of knowledge that awaits!

Neurological Basis: Entering the depths of neuroscience, we delve into the neurological basis of body language. How does the brain translate a seemingly insignificant shrug or certain facial expressions into a web of meaningful information? The answers lie in the intricate workings of our nervous system. Renowned neuroscientist Paul MacLean proposed a model known as the 'triune brain theory', which breaks down the human brain into three distinct parts: the reptilian complex, the limbic system, and the neocortex. Each plays a crucial role in our non-verbal communication.

The 'reptilian complex', tasked with the most rudimentary body functions like heart rate and temperature control, is also responsible for some instinctual body language. Ever felt a sudden chill run down your spine when you are frightened? Or the pounding of your heart when attracted to someone? These involuntary reactions are guided by our reptilian brain.

Then we have the 'limbic system', the emotional center of our brain. It's where body language starts to get a bit more sophisticated. Peer into the eyes of someone laughing heartily - the spark you see comes from their limbic system. It's that spark which gives away the authenticity of their laughter, differentiating it from a forced, polite chuckle. The limbic brain guides us through the world of emotional expressions, nudging our faces to frown, smile, grimace, or glimmer depending on what we feel.

Finally, enter the 'neocortex', the most evolved part of the human brain. Control of subtler gestures, recognition of complex patterns, empathy, all come down to the neocortex. Consider a person raising an eyebrow knowingly, or someone mirroring your posture in a conversation – the neocortex is at play. It's what interprets these high-level signs and uses them to build a richer understanding of the social environment.

Let's talk about mirror neurons, a delightful nugget of neuroscience that has been revolutionizing our understanding of body language. Discovered by Italian scientist Giacomo Rizzolatti, these particular neurons fire up not just when we perform an action, but also when we see someone else perform that same action. Essentially, they help us mirror others' actions internally, leading to empathy and aiding in nonverbal communication. Think about the last time you yawned seeing someone do the same. That's your mirror neurons in action!

Another significant part of the brain when discussing body language is the amygdala, often referred to as the body's 'alarm system'. Having a strong connection with the limbic system, it activates our fight, flight, or freeze responses during stressful situations and may force our bodies to leak out signals of distress through our body language. Sweating, fast breathing, or foot-tapping are all under its command.

Let's not forget that body language is a two-way street - our brain doesn't just control our non-verbal signals, but also deciphers the ones we receive. The 'fusiform face area' (FFA) in our neocortex helps us recognize and interpret faces, an essential part of non-verbal communication.

What does all this neurological talk mean for you? Understanding the neurological basis of body language can provide a solid foundation for consistent and accurate interpretations. And it can do more than that. It can help you understand why people often have similar reactions to situations and how emotions can be "contagious". So next time when you're in a conversation, remember, your brain is doing the heavy lifting, weaving the narrative from a myriad of subtle cues and signals it picks up from others.

Remember, our understanding of the body-brain link in communication is not yet exhaustive – we're still exploring, researching, and making discoveries. But, the fascinating findings made so far already carry deep implications for how we perceive and utilize body language to our advantage.

Understanding the neurological basis of body language is not about diagnosing brain activity or becoming a neuroscientist, it's about getting an insightful edge in conversations or negotiations. By knowing how our brain interacts with our body in communicating feelings and intentions, you're better equipped to read the signs, anticipate reactions, and take the lead in interactions.

Role of Hormones Now, moving on from the neurological basis, let's dive into the role of hormones in deciphering body language. The hormones in our body are invisible messengers carrying out a myriad of necessary functions. They've got a subtle, yet undeniable influence on our body language and subsequently, our non-verbal communication patterns.

Let's kick things off with serotonin, a hormone primarily linked with feelings of happiness and well-being. If someone's body language is open and animatedly engaging, there's a decent chance they've got a healthy dose of serotonin at play. In contrast, lower levels can lead to a more subdued, reserved non-verbal expression. Ain't no rulebook to this, but keep an eye out for signs like this, it can help shed some light on what's going on beneath the surface.

Another hormone to take note of is cortisol, widely recognized as the 'stress hormone.' High levels of cortisol are often reflected in body language signals like rapid movements, fidgeting, or even a closed-off posture. So, if you notice someone consistently exhibiting such behaviors, it might be an indication of heightened stress or anxiety levels. In these situations, empathetic and supportive communication can go a long way.

Moving on, testosterone. Often associated with dominance and aggression, this hormone's presence can manifest in assertive and confrontational body language. Lack of eye contact or an overly aggressive posture could be indicative of escalated testosterone levels. Be mindful, though, as misreading this body language can lead to unnecessary conflicts - it's always good to tread with caution.

Then there's oxytocin, better known as the 'love hormone.' Oxytocin can be a game-changer in the way we read body language. It generally elicits behaviors of bonding, increased eye contact, and contentment. If you notice comfortable and relaxed body language with prolonged eye contact, oxytocin might just have joined the party.

Another hormone worth mentioning here is adrenaline. Commonly associated with the body's fight-or-flight response, adrenaline can rev things up, leading to rapid gestures, dilated pupils, and possibly nervous behaviors. If the signs point towards a surge in adrenaline, it might be wise to diffuse the situation or provide reassurances if applicable.

Last but not least, dopamine, the 'pleasure hormone.' It's associated with pleasure, reward, and motivation. High dopamine levels can project enthusiastic body language, increased engagement, and responsiveness. Dopamine-influenced body language could be used as a benchmark to gauge if a conversation is heading in a favorable direction.

In a nutshell, hormones, these invisible forces of nature, not only shape our inner feelings but also subtly color our non-verbal cues. By keeping an eye out for these hormone-driven signs and signals, you'll be adding yet another layer of depth to your body language interpretation skills. Keep in mind though, reading hormonal signs in body language isn't a definitive science. It's more or less like connecting dots, weaving together clues into a coherent picture.

Remember, being mindful of others' body language can provide you with invaluable insights about their emotional state, and therefore, how best to communicate with them. By understanding the role of hormones and their impact on body language, you can better foresee other's reactions, adjust your approach, or even predict their next move.

Now that we've looked into the roles of both neurological signals and hormones, we can move on to explore the fascinating field of psychophysiology. Get ready to delve even deeper into the compelling world of body language and non-verbal communication.

Understanding Psychophysiology can be central to mastering body language reading. But what is psychophysiology? Simply put, it's the branch of psychology concerned with the physiological bases of psychological processes. It studies the relationship between our psychological experiences and our bodily reactions, asserting that we can't separate 'mind' from 'body.'

So, how does this all tie in with body language? Well, our physiological responses often reveal our inner feelings before we're conscious of them. For example, when someone is stressed, their body may produce more sweat, their heart rate may increase, or their facial expressions may change subtly. All of these are physical expressions of their psychological condition, which can be detected and interpreted as body language.

Consider our instinctual 'fight or flight' response. When we're confronted with a threat, real or perceived, our bodies automatically respond — our muscles tense, our heart rate quickens, and adrenaline is released. This isn't a frivolous reaction; it's a set of signals telling us to react — to run from the danger or fight it head on. We can see this clearly in body language as aggressive or defensive stances, rigid postures, clenched fists, or wide eyes.

But let's not get too caught up in the major reactions. Psychophysiology plays an essential role in subtle changes too. Ever noticed a quickened blink rate when someone's nervous? Or dilated pupils when they're interested? How about an increase in personal space when they're uncomfortable? These subtle signs are where the art of reading body language pays dividends, offering valuable insight into the emotional states and thoughts of others.

It's also important to remember that psychophysiological responses vary from person to person. There's a certain art to interpreting these cues. What might be a telltale sign of anxiety for one person might just be a tick or meaningless gesture for another. As a body language reader, it's essential to understand this variability and remain adaptable.

Then, there's the matter of context. Context is everything when it comes to interpreting body language. The environment, situation, and people involved all contribute to the psychophysiological responses. For instance, what might be seen as a gesture of disinterest (say a crossed arm) in a business meeting might just be a way to keep warm at an outdoor event.

Assuming you've grasped hormonal influence, it's impressive to see how our hormone levels can shape our psychophysiological response. Think of the hormone oxytocin, often known as the 'love hormone.' When it's released during moments of intimacy or connection, our body language may soften, expressing openness and warmth. Other hormones like cortisol (the stress hormone) and adrenaline are associated with more defensive or aggressive signals.

Certain facial expressions tied to specific emotions are universal across cultures. That's no accident. It's driven by our psychophysiology. An expression of shock, anger, or happiness triggers similar facial muscle responses in people no matter where they are from.

As we wrap up this section, let's highlight the ultimate goal: to help you become more attuned to the nuances of body language by understanding the psychophysiological roots behind them. By realizing our bodies are not just passive vehicles, but participants in each interaction, you'll be one step closer to effectively reading and interpreting the body language of those around you.

Chapter 3:
Reading Emotional States

As we delve further, it's essential to understand the role emotion plays in our physical behaviors. We're all familiar with the triumphant raise of the arms when we're feeling victorious or the furrowed brow during a troublesome thought, but let's dig deeper. Happiness, sadness, and anger are often presented in grand, unmistakable gestures, but it's crucial not to miss the less prominent signs - those slight upturns of the lips, the subtle drop of the eyes, or the almost imperceptible tensing of the jaw. Now fear, surprise, and disgust, on the other hand, can sometimes be more elusive; often masked or misinterpreted, learning to accurately identify the flinches, gasps, or grimaces that are tied to these emotions can truly turn a good body language decoder into a great one. Emotions, often seen as the heart's language, profoundly impact our body language as they unconsciously leak information about our true feelings and mental state. Recognizing and understanding these emotional states isn't just a neat party trick, it's the key to more profound empathy, smoother conversations, and ultimately, stronger connections.

Recognizing Happiness, Sadness, and Anger

Our journey into understanding the language of the body continues with an exploration of three fundamental emotions: happiness, sadness, and anger. Each has its unique physical manifestation, subtly speaking volumes if you know to take note of the signs. Let's delve into the world of emotional states and discover how to identify these feelings.

Often, happiness is the easiest emotion to recognize. The hallmarks of genuine joy include a wide, unrestrained smile that crinkles the eyes - a clear indication that the pleasure isn't merely being faked for social nicety. The posture tends to be open and relaxed, and there's often a notable 'glow' in the eyes. You might also see relaxed body language, like uncrossed arms and legs, suggesting comfort and ease in the current situation.

Look out for mimicking behaviors too. When you're truly happy and feeling in sync with someone, you'll unconsciously mirror their movements. Remember that sometimes, the indicators of joy can vary across different regions, cultures, and even from person to person.

Contrast this with the signs of sadness. The physical signs accompanying this emotion are often more subtle and vary widely from person to person. Downcast eyes, a lowering of the head, and a feeble or fake smile are all common indicators of sadness. Slumped shoulders and a lethargic, sluggish demeanor can also point to inner despair. A person might also withdraw, both emotionally and physically, for example, crossing their arms or legs to subconsciously shield themselves from emotional pain.

Avoid misreading the signs of sadness, while some may hide their feelings behind forced smiles, others might withdraw into themselves. The key here is to pay attention to general body language, as sadness often permeates every aspect of a person's demeanor, from their reduced eye contact to less physical movement.

Moving on, the third emotion we're exploring is anger. Anger, like happiness and sadness, has distinct physical signs. The expressions could range from the obvious – like clenching of jaws or fists, furrowed brows and flushing of the face; to the very subtle – an icy, fixed gaze, terse tone of voice, rapid speech, or restlessness.

Decoding Silence

Be aware, not all displays of anger are loud and explosive. Some individuals may stew in silence, keeping their resentment under wraps. However, even suppressed anger tends to show up in body language. Look for tightly controlled movements, a rigid posture, and intense eye contact. They might also maintain an imposing or dominating body position — such as standing over you — as a subconscious attempt at intimidation.

Remember, detection of anger can be vital in preventing harmful situations. If you see these signs, it's probably best to stay calm and to steer clear of upsetting topics if possible.

Recognition of these emotions isn't about judgment but understanding. It's about tuning into people's feelings and responding with empathy. However, bear in mind that these are just general guidelines. Remember, every person is unique in their expression of these emotions.

Another important note: the absence of these signs doesn't necessarily signify the lack of these emotions. It could also be a mastery of masking genuine feelings, a common practice in many social and professional settings. Having a keen eye to spot these small indications can give you an edge in navigating social situations with grace and ease.

Consequently, with careful observation and a dash of intuition, you can unlock a world of understanding not just others, but yourself better. After all, our body language is merely an external reflection of our internal emotional state. And by recognizing these signs in ourselves, we might sometimes uncover emotions we didn't initially realize we were experiencing.

In the next section, we'll look at the subtler, often overlooked emotions - fear, surprise, and disgust. Like happiness, sadness, and anger, these hold a wealth of information you can use to decode the language of the body further.

Ready to dig deeper? Let's continue our journey into understanding the wordless language of the body! The mastery of reading emotional states isn't just about identifying feelings but appreciating the story our bodies unconsciously narrate about our emotional landscape. The more we understand, the richer our interactions become as we unravel the art of empathetic connection in our everyday interactions.

Unmasking Fear, Surprise, and Disgust

Body language is a fascinating arena which offers a panoply of signals ranging from ubiquitous behavior to subtle nuances. This section will delve deep into identifying the landscape of fear, surprise, and disgust through nonverbal cues. These emotions, often layered under a facade, can be tricky to detect but with the right understanding, you'll be better equipped to unmask these feelings. Let's start decoding.

First, let's understand fear. Fear manifests itself in myriad ways. Comprehending fear is pivotal in recognizing a person's discomfort, stress, anxiety, and empathy. Watch out for wide-open eyes and raised eyebrows, or the fight, flight, or freeze response, where the body tenses up or tries to physically move away from the source of fear.

Additionally, subtle cues like rapid breathing, trembling of hands, lip biting, face touching or averting eye contact can also indicate fear. Crossed arms might suggest self-soothing or protection, and even in speech you might observe stuttering or speech inconsistencies.

Next, let's explore surprise, an emotion that's often transient and can quickly morph into another emotion like joy or anger. Identifying genuine surprise is important, as it's a spontaneous reaction to unexpected events and people often don't have enough time to mask it.

When surprised, a person's eyes dart wide open for a moment and the eyebrows rapidly shoot up. Other facial muscles may momentarily freeze, and sometimes the mouth goes open for a split second. Afterward, depending upon the cause of the surprise, the facial expressions change to reflect the actual emotional response to the event, which could be happiness, annoyance, or even fear.

Often confused with surprise is the emotion of shock, but these are not the same. Shock is usually a prolonged state and often coupled with complete dismay or disbelief. The body language associated with shock includes a slack jaw, widened eyes, and a glazed-over look.

Lastly, we explore disgust, literally a gut reaction, which is a primal response to something distasteful or unpleasant. It's hard to fake and often comes across clearly.

A telltale is the classic facial grimace – the nose wrinkles, the upper lip may raise, and sometimes, the tongue sticks out. This is something universal, seen from the tribes in the Amazon to the skyscrapers of New York. Along with the facial expressions, the person might physically back away or shield themselves from the offending item or situation.

However, remember that body language is as much an art as it is a science. While these signals give a solid starting point in understanding fear, surprise, and disgust, they are not definitive rules set in stone. It is the combination of these signals, the context, and the understanding of individuals' baseline behaviors, which will truly open windows to their souls.

Furthermore, cultural backgrounds can have a profound impact on the display and interpretation of body language. What may be considered a sign of fear in one culture may not hold true in another. It's essential to factor this in when 'reading' an individual.

Also, realize that people might, consciously or unconsciously, mimic or suppress their body language. Deception can play a major role, especially when the stakes are high, like in business negotiations or high tension situations.

Decoding these non-verbal signals requires patience and practice. It's a game of piecing together a puzzle, looking out for mismatches and inconsistencies. The more you tune in, the more sensitive you become to even the slightest changes. That's the beauty of body language - it never lies, and it always speaks the truth.

Remember, your objective is not to turn body language reading into an interrogation tool, but to use it to foster better personal and professional relationships. It's about making people comfortable, understanding their fears and concerns, and acting empathetically. So, as you progress in this fascinating journey, let these insights guide you into becoming more astute observers and listeners, but above all, better communicators.

In the next section, we will further delve into subtle cues that often go unnoticed and comprehend common misconceptions. The premise remains the same - The body speaks volumes, and the more you listen, the more you learn.

Identifying Subtle Cues Now that we have had a good look at the basic expressions of emotions, let's dig a little deeper and investigate subtler signals people often send. These are the little tells that can reveal a person's true feelings, thoughts, or intentions, even when they are trying to hide them. Identifying these subtle cues, also known as microexpressions, can be likened to reading a secret language, utterly hidden from the untrained eye.

Certainly, these cues are brief, often lasting only a fraction of a second. For example, a quick tightening around the eyes can suggest doubt or disbelief, while a brief touch to the nose might signal deception or uncertainty. The challenge is not just recognizing these fleeting signals, but correctly interpreting them as well. They are complex, multifaceted, and strongly influenced by an individual's culture, upbringing, and personal habits.

It might not be obvious, but hands can be very expressive too. Clenched fists, for instance, may indicate tension or frustration. Rubbing hands together often suggests anticipation, while a single, short nod might signal approval or acknowledgement. On the flip side, a vigorous, repeated nod could mean someone is impatient or trying to hurry the conversation along.

Does the person you're talking to barely blink? When people are genuinely interested or focused, they often blink less. Rapid blinking, conversely, can signal distress or discomfort. How about eye contact? Consistent, direct eye contact can show interest and engagement, but beware, overly prolonged eye contact can be perceived as aggressive or intimidating.

Let's talk about posture. Arms crossed over the chest are generally interpreted as defensive or closed off. But make sure not to jump to conclusions! If the room is a bit chilly or the person is physically uncomfortable, they might cross their arms for those reasons instead. And here is a fun tip: too much nodding can imply that the person is impatient and wants you to speed things up.

The position of a person's feet can deliver insightful cues as well. If someone's feet are pointed towards the door while they are talking to you, it might indicate they're itching to leave. Shuffling feet often signify nervousness or discomfort. Cultivate the habit of observing a person's whole body language, not just their facial expressions or gestures.

On the verbal front, notice how people speak. A rise in pitch at the end of a sentence can indicate a question, doubt, or uncertainty, even if the sentence isn't structured as a question. Rapid, frenzied speech could denote excitement or nervousness, while slow, measured tones could suggest the speaker is trying to control the conversation or dominate the interaction.

Are they mirroring your body language? This is often a sign of admiration and that they are trying to build rapport with you. When people are comfortable with each other, they often unconsciously mimic each other's gestures, expressions, and posture. So, if someone starts to mirror your actions, take it as a good sign.

To effectively interpret these signals, it's important to not consider each cue in isolation but rather to consider them as part of a larger communication context. Are the words in sync with the non-verbal cues? Are the facial expressions, hand gestures, and posture all telling the same story? This holistic approach is key to accurately decoding the subtle cues in body language.

Common Misconceptions Body language is often viewed as a secret decoder ring to the soul. Unlike spoken language, we're conditioned to believe that body language is a world of universal, unchanging 'tells.' However, few things could be further from the truth. The notion that positive non-verbal signals are identical across cultures or even amongst individuals within the same culture is quite misleading. Interpreting body language is not as simple as declaring crossed arms a sign of defensiveness or smiling an indication of happiness. These cues can mean entirely different things depending on the context.

One of the most widespread misconceptions is that lack of eye contact always signifies deceit or evasion. Truth be told, some people avert their gaze when they're nervous, anxious, or even when heavily contemplating a topic. It may be a sign of someone attempting to recall a memory, rather than formulating a lie. The reverse belief, that good eye contact is a sign of honesty or confidence, similarly ignores individual and cultural variations.

Believe it or not, many people assume that closed body language—like crossed arms—always implies negative emotions or disinterest. However, this isn't always the case; it might simply be a habit or a way that person feels comfortable. Some individuals might cross their arms because they're cold or because that position is physically comfortable for them.

Another misconception worth busting is the constant emphasis on confident body language signs, like standing tall or taking up space. While such signals might demonstrate self-assuredness in some individuals, others might naturally physically express themselves in that manner. It doesn't necessarily mean they're particularly confident or dominant. It might simply be sociocultural conditioning or a learned behavior.

In conclusion, while body language can provide some cues into a person's feelings or intentions, it is crucial to remember that these are just potential clues and not definitive answers. It's a complex language with its own syntax, semantics, and dialects, varying based on countless factors like personality, cultural background, and context. As we continue exploring body language, always bear in mind that it's less of an exact science and more of an art, tied to the nuanced dynamics of human interaction.

Chapter 4:
Body Language in Everyday Interactions

Strolling through a bustling street, navigating arduous office politics, or settling in for a cozy dinner with friends - everyday interactions are rife with opportunities for non-verbal communication to leap into play. Observing and deciphering these silent conversational partners gives us an edge in harnessing the power of connection, breaking barriers and drawing people in. A subtle nod from an acquaintance can speak volumes about their comfort level while a colleague slumping in a chair during a meeting may reveal a lack of interest or motivation. You see, it's in these routine situations that body language seems to have the most profound impact. It's not just about broad gestures or accentuated facial expressions, but subtler actions - an averted gaze, a light touch, or a crossed leg. These are the building blocks of a non-verbal dialogue that impact relationships and outcomes in various social and professional contexts. As we delve into the nitty-gritty, consider how body language shapes your interactions and the untold stories that reveal themselves once we begin to 'listen' with our eyes.

Body Language in Social Situations

The second you walk through a room, a story is being told. Sounds dramatic, right? But, quite literally, your body language is narrating a non-verbal account about you before any words even leave your mouth. It's paging through your anxiety or comfort, openness or closemindedness, interest or boredom. More intriguingly, it's happening without you even noticing.

But here's the secret sauce: you can indeed influence this silent chronicle. With a solid understanding of your body language and that of others, a mundane social interaction could become a superb opportunity to connect on a deeper level. It can be intimidating, yes, but it's about as intimidating as learning how to ride a bike. It might seem daunting at first, but once you get the hang of it, you'll be cruising.

Let's start with open and closed body language. Open body language includes actions like keeping your arms unfolded, maintaining steady eye contact, and angling your body towards the person you're interacting with. This type of body language is inviting, conveying warmth and engagement in the conversation.

On the flipside, closed body language - crossing your arms, turning away, or consistently looking around - sends a message of disinterest or discomfort. It's as if you're building a barrier between you and the other person. These subtle, often unconscious actions can drastically influence the tone and outcome of an interaction.

Beyond openness and closeness, our bodies help signal interest. The amount of interest we show toward someone can be gauged by our level of mirroring. It's the subconscious mimicking of another person's body language. It sounds strange, but it's a natural phenomenon that occurs when we're genuinely invested in another person or their conversation.

But wait, it's a two-way street! Not only can you demonstrate interest within a chat, but you can also sense if the interest is mutual. Are you leaning into the conversation and finding that the other person is doing the same? That's mirroring.

The proximity between you and the other individual also reveals a great deal of information. Similar to how animals claim their personal space, as humans, we also have a bubble around us indicating our comfort level with others in the vicinity. If someone inches closer, they're likely comfortable with you. If they're perpetually backing away, they might need some more, well, personal space.

We're not all Chopins of body language naturally—some of us might be more on the deafening-end of a recorder. The good news? It doesn't need to stay that way. We can tune our abilities with a bit of patience and practice. Start consciously noticing your own body language in your daily life. Are you using closed body language with people you're comfortable with? Have you mirrored someone's posture without even realizing it?

After noting your own behaviors, begin observing those around you. People watching isn't just a way to pass the time - in this case, it's active research. See if you can spot the open or closed body language, the mirror effect, or the delicate dance of personal space in others.

Delving into others' body language might feel a bit like peeping into their personal diary, but remember, this isn't about getting the scoop on their innermost secrets. It's about enriching interactions and creating that connection that sticks. We are social creatures, after all, and understanding each other on a deeper level is how we form meaningful relationships.

So there you have it. Grasping body language in social situations isn't about analyzing every single tic or blink, but rather learning to take a step back and see the bigger picture. It's more of an art than an exact science. Just like any art, it'll take time to master. But once you get a grip on it, you will begin to unravel the layered dialogues going on beneath the spoken words.

But one size doesn't fit all, right? These cues can be influenced by cultural differences, personal idiosyncrasies, and previous experiences. It will take time and practice to get it right. But you've taken the first step in this lovely dance. Go forth and conquer those social situations with your newfound knowledge. Trust me, once you open your eyes to this, there's no going back. You're on your way to becoming a maestro of social relations, all thanks to the silent yet powerful language of the body.

Body Language in Professional Environment

The world of work is a social arena, a place where different players come together, with varied goals and ambitions. Even though communication in a professional environment often relies heavily on spoken and written words, body language plays a critical role. It acts as the undercurrent of all interactions, subtly complementing or occasionally contradicting verbal exchanges. Understanding body language in a professional setting can provide valuable insights into the dynamics of the workplace.

Most business interactions take place in the context of meetings. In these scenarios, body language reveals much more than terms of a deal or strategic ideas being shared. The direction of people's feet, for instance, commonly indicates their interest. A pair of feet turned towards the exit could signal eagerness to leave, while directed towards a person suggests engagement in the conversation.

Equally critical in assessing engagement is a person's posture. Someone who's hunched over or continuously fiddling with objects may not be fully invested in the meeting, whereas someone sitting upright and attentive indicates enthusiasm and concentration. This could also highlight their perceived importance of the topic or speaker.

Moreover, mirroring body language suggests rapport and agreement. On the flip side, if people are consistently not mirroring each other's gestures and postures, it may indicate disagreement or friction. Understanding this dynamic can help navigate potentially tricky situations before they escalate.

Nods and gestures carry critical non-verbal messages. Rapid nodding may suggest impatience while slower nods communicate understanding and agreement. Similarly, open-handed gestures usually convey honesty and openness, while closed fists or crossed arms could reflect defensiveness or hostility. Knowing these subtleties can provide an edge in communication, enhancing overall effectiveness in professional settings.

Professional presentations are another scenario where body language speaks volumes. A presenter exuding confidence, marked by steady eye contact, relaxed stance, and controlled gestures makes a stronger impression and can better engage the audience's attention.

Evasion of direct eye contact or the frequent use of filler words like 'um,' 'er,' and 'like' can make a presenter appear unsure. In the highly competitive corporate world, such signals can jeopardize credibility, and must be avoided.

Body language also affects audience engagement. A responsive audience would usually lean forward, maintain consistent eye contact, and nod at intervals. If members seem distracted or unresponsive, the presenter might want to adjust their delivery, content, or pace to regain attention.

Moreover, the power dynamics in the workplace can be unveiled through body language. For instance, those higher up the power ladder will often adopt larger postures and occupy more space than their subordinates. They also tend to engage in more eye contact while speaking to emphasize their control over the conversation.

Expressions of dominance can sometimes be subtle. A person may use something as minor as a prolonged handshake or direct body orientation to establish dominance or superiority over others. Recognizing these patterns allows individuals to understand the power dynamics within the workplace and adjust their behavior accordingly.

The implications of misreading body language professionally can be quite profound. An interpreted slight could lead to resentment or visible discomfort could be misconstrued as disinterest. These misinterpretations can hamper team dynamics, and make negotiations and business dealings more complicated.

The ability to read body language correctly within the professional environment can be highly beneficial. It can positively impact networking and negotiation, team building, management, sales tactics, customer interactions, and more. Such keen understanding boosts the efficiency of communication and enhances overall professionalism.

In conclusion, body language is like an ongoing conversation, often revealing what words do not intentionally express. In professional settings, understanding these unspoken hints becomes a valuable asset, influencing perceptions, aiding in conflict resolution, and ultimately facilitating success in the workplace.

As we undergo this journey of exploring body language in depth, the next chapter will delve into an exciting and insightful area: predicting intentions through body language. How can you decode someone's perceived aggression or interest just by their non-verbal cues? Stick with us to find out!

In Meetings - Body language in meetings can be a powerful indicator of a person's thoughts, feelings, and intentions. Whether it's a simple catch-up or a high-stake board meeting, understanding how to read body language signals can offer valuable insights into the dynamics of any discussion.

During meetings, facial expressions seem magnified due to the close proximity and the focused nature of interactions. A slight wrinkle of the nose, barely-there frown, or a brief nod might give away one's unvoiced thoughts. Recognizing these small, nuanced facial expressions can provide you a clearer understanding of a person's opinion on an issue that may not be verbally expressed.

In addition to facial expressions, gestures and postures also give away a lot in a meeting setup. A relaxed posture could suggest comfort or contentment with the ongoing discussion. Conversely, defensive postures such as crossed arms might reveal discomfort, disagreement, or resistance. Observing these non-verbal cues can help you gauge the overall mood and adjust your approach to better tackle contentious issues.

Let's not forget eye contact, which plays a pivotal role in meetings. The frequency and length of eye contact can suggest engagement, interest, and confidence. However, avoidant eye contact or excessive blinking might hint at anxiety, discomfort, or dishonesty. Thus, understanding these signals can offer you a deeper understanding of the person across the table.

Space, or the lack of it, speaks volumes too. People often subconsciously manipulate the physical distance between themselves and others based on their comfort level. A person leaning in during a conversation signals enthusiasm and interest. On the other hand, leaning back or moving away can signal disinterest or discomfort. Considering this spatial aspect of body language can help establish the right level of comfort and rapport in a meeting.

Hand movements also offer significant clues. You may observe that many people talk with their hands. For some, it's a method of translating their thought process into a visual format. You might notice someone tapping their fingers when they are impatient or clasping their hands when they feel defensive. Mirroring these gestures subtly, when appropriate, can convey empathy and understanding, aiding in building stronger connections.

And it's not just about what others are conveying. Being aware of your own body language during meetings is equally critical. By showcasing open body language (like open palms, maintaining eye contact, and nodding at the right moments), you can instill trust and encourage open conversation. Conversely, you may inadvertently send out signals of impatience or disinterest (like repeatedly checking your watch or phone), which might hinder open communication.

Understanding body language in meetings is not about scrutinizing every single movement but forming a holistic image based on various non-verbal cues. Remember, body language interpretation is not an exact science but an art that requires a keen eye, a clear understanding of context, and, most importantly, respect for the individual's personal space and comfort.

Mastering the subtleties of body language in meetings doesn't just help in predicting others' behaviors or thoughts, but can also enhance your own communication skills. It arms you with knowledge to express yourself better and at the same time, respect and understand the unvoiced thoughts of others, making every meeting productive and comfortable for all parties involved.

During Presentations, understanding body language can be particularly influential. When you're delivering a presentation, you're not just conveying information through your words. The way you carry yourself and express non-verbally can either amplify your message or detract from its impact. Simultaneously, the body language of your audience can provide immediate feedback, helping you to enhance your communication in real-time.

At the start of any presentation, it's essential to secure a commanding presence. You can achieve this through body language that conveys confidence and authority. Stand tall with your shoulders back and face the audience squarely rather than at an angle. Moreover, use open gestures, such as spreading your arms to indicate inclusivity and engage the audience. This openness invites connection and shows you're in control and comfortable with the arena.

Eye contact plays a pivotal role during presentations, helping you connect with your audience on a personal level. If the crowd is relatively small, make a point to establish direct eye contact with numerous individuals. In larger groups, you can sweep your gaze across the room to create a more generalized connection. Avoiding eye contact may make you appear untrustworthy or nervous, which can undermine your message.

However, it's not just about your body language; the audience's body language also matters. Observing your crowd's non-verbal cues can serve as a valuable feedback mechanism, enabling you to tailor your delivery. If you spot signs of engagement, such as forward-leaning postures, nodding heads, or focused faces, it means you're doing well. On the flip side, if you see crossed arms, diverted gazes, or individuals leaning back, it might call for a change of pace or approach.

In conclusion, harnessing body language during presentations doesn't just enhance your communication but also helps identify areas for improvement. Personalize your body language to match your presentation style while keeping a keen eye on your audience's non-verbal cues to gauge their engagement level. Remember, the goal is not just to read body language but to meaningfully respond to it, creating a constant loop of reflective communication during your presentation.

Chapter 5:
Predicting Intentions through Body Language

As we deepen our dive into the world of body language, we find ourselves at an intriguing touchstone: predicting intentions. Seems a bit like mind-reading, doesn't it? But to paraphrase a saying, language is not only about words - it's also about gesture, posture, facial expressions and much more. Intentions, once shrouded, can become crystal clear, provided you know how to keenly observe and interpret the subtle signs. Let's pretend you're having an enthusiastic discussion with a work colleague; they're leaning towards you, their eyes are wide and responsive, and their hands are animatedly emphasizing their points. Are they passionately agreeing with you, or masterfully picking a fight? That's where understanding aggressive and defensive body language patterns comes in handy. Similarly, an unwavering gaze or a casual touch during a conversation could be signals of desire or interest. All you need to do is read the signs correctly and in context. Not to forget those quick hallway exchanges with an acquaintance that leave you wondering about the undercurrents. What if you could not merely survive such interactions but actually thrive, by identifying subtleties in body language? This thought might be overwhelming, but trust me, once you grasp these aspects, predicting people's intentions throws open a fascinating gateway to more meaningful interactions.

Understanding Aggressive and Defensive Responses

Let's delve into the realm of aggressive and defensive body language. These are vital reactions for us to understand and recognize, as they often reveal conflicting intentions, emotions, or states of discomfort.

Firstly, it's important to understand that aggression doesn't always translate to physical hostility. Often, it can be a manifestation of mental or emotional aggression. This type of aggression is typically exhibited through more covert signs, such as a clenched jaw, narrowed eyes, or intrusive personal space.

The clenched jaw, in particular, signifies inner tension and restraint; an effort to contain one's anger or frustration. Similarly, narrowed eyes are typically associated with suspicion, hostility, or focus. When someone is intruding on your personal space aggressively, it usually indicates a desire for dominance and control.

Defensive responses, on the other hand, are remarkably different. They communicate a sense of vulnerability or threat. It's like seeing a hedgehog roll into a ball; it's an attempt to protect oneself. Defensive behaviors are often distinguished through signs such as crossed arms, minimal eye contact, or backing away.

Crossed arms are like a physical barrier, a subconscious attempt to protect oneself from perceived danger or discomfort. Not making eye contact communicates a lack of confidence or discomfort, often suggesting a desire to avoid interaction. And, of course, physically moving back or away from a conversation shows a clear intention to create distance and protect personal space.

However, it's essential to understand that these signs aren't conclusive evidence of aggression or defense. They are part of a broader context. We need to perceive their body language in the context of the overall situation and environment, alongside the dialogue and other non-verbal cues.

Let's consider an example - if someone is speaking to you while constantly looking over your shoulder, it might seem as though they're not interested. However, what if they're at a bustling train station, it's likely they're just anxiously checking for their train arrival. In this case, the environment, not the person, is creating a sense of urgency and redirecting their attention.

Similarly, if a person is making minimal eye contact in a professional environment, it doesn't necessarily mean they're not confident. They may just be focusing on their work or notes. Understanding the context will make a world of difference in your interpretation of their body language.

Besides, we should not forget cultural differences. What might be perceived as aggressive in one culture can mean something entirely different in another. For example, maintaining direct eye contact is commonplace in Western cultures. It suggests honesty and openness. But in other cultures, prolonged eye contact may be viewed as disrespectful or aggressive.

Therefore, while understanding aggressive and defensive body language is helpful in gauging someone's intentions or feelings, we should refrain from making snap judgments. Merely because a person displays one or two of these cues doesn't cement them as being aggressive or defensive. It should be considered as a piece of a larger puzzle.

When in doubt, look for clusters of signals. If a person is displaying multiple signs of aggression or defense, it's more likely that they're feeling that way. Crossed arms alone may not suggest defense, but when paired with minimal eye contact and backing away, it paints a reasonably solid picture of defensiveness.

Ultimately, understanding aggressive and defensive responses necessitate empathy and keen observation. It's about viewing the entire picture rather than getting myopic about specific signals. It's about understanding the person beyond what they're verbally communicating and truly tuning in to their non-verbal cues.

But as always, these observations are not meant for manipulative purposes. They're tools to foster understanding, build bridges, and promote honest communication. So let's use this knowledge to understand each other better and create a more empathetic society!

Deciphering Desire and Interest

Our journey into the realm of body language continues, as we venture into deciphering desire and interest. It's fascinating to realize the numerous non-verbal cues we communicate daily without even being consciously aware. Let's learn to decipher these significant signals.

The body provides an array of signals that denote desire and interest, starting from the eyes. Eye contact displays attentiveness and interest in a conversation. People who fancy someone can't help but maintain prolonged eye contact. Also, dilated pupils indicate a heightened interest and is a natural response to being attracted to something or someone.

Revealing interest goes beyond the eyes. You'll notice that when someone is attracted to another person, they tend to lean in during conversations. Their body unconsciously moves closer, attempting to bridge the gap, and conveys an interest in wanting to be in the person's space.

A significant indicator of interest or desire in conversations is active listening, portrayed through body language like nodding, an open posture, and mimicking the person's actions. This phenomenon known as mirroring is a subtle sign of interest as it shows a desire to connect on a deeper level.

An often overlooked sign of interest is when individuals point their feet towards the person they're interested in. This subconscious action happens despite the direction the body or face might be pointing and communicates the desire to move closer or to follow the direction of interest.

Touch is another powerful communicator of desire and interest. A gentle touch on the arm during a conversation can express excitement or agreement, while more intimate touches, like brushing a hair strand off someone's face, might indicate a greater level of interest or romantic intentions.

When a person is interested, they might also reveal their palms or wrists more often during a conversation. This gesture suggests openness and trust, showing a desire to connect. Even the way someone grips a mug or holds a pen might be an unconscious show of aim or interest.

The way we speak, the tone of our voice also plays a key role in expressing interest. Someone interested in you might subtly adjust their speech volume, pitch, or speed to match yours, indicating a form of empathy and connection.

Smiling is another universal sign of interest and fondness. Genuine smiles, the ones that light up the eyes and are seen beyond the mere extension of lips, denote genuine pleasure and interest. It's infectious and usually reciprocated when the interest is mutual, forming a loop of positive reinforcement.

Interest recognition isn't just about single cues though, it's about the big picture. It's about understanding and scoring the different pieces together. Delving deeper into understanding body language gives you that edge, that ability to read and interpret the story a person's body is telling beyond their words.

All of these signals have a simple aim – to draw closer to the object of interest or desire. Mastering the ability to read these signals can not only improve your interpersonal relationships but also help you avoid misunderstandings and foster stronger connections.

Our ability to accurately decipher desire and interest through body language hinges on our understanding of cultural and personal differences as well. What might stand for interest in one culture could denote respect in another. Personal space ranges vary from person to person too. Being attuned to these small differences is part of the complexity and beauty of body language.

As we become more adept at noticing and interpreting these subtle non-verbal cues, we open up a new channel of communication. This skill can provide insights into someone's thoughts or feelings that they might not explicitly express or even be consciously aware of, enhancing our interactions manifold.

Deciphering the signs of desire and interest can feel like tackling a new language. But with practice, you can get to a point where you are fluent in this non-verbal communication and are capable of reading the unsaid expressions of intentions and emotions. So keep practicing, and keep learning, because the world of body language never stops speaking!

Decoding a Quick Conversation with an Acquaintance

Imagine this: You're at a social gathering, and you bump into an acquaintance. The conversation begins on a pleasant note, but something seems off. Their words suggest interest, but their body language is telling a different story. In this section, we're going to dive deeper into this complex dance, specifically focusing on how to decode the intention behind the short, seemingly meaningless conversations you might have with an acquaintance.

Initially, a smile is a good start, but is it reaching their eyes? Or is it a tight, polite smile that indicates disinterest? Another tell-tale sign is their eye contact. Are they maintaining it, or does it stray elsewhere? People tend to maintain eye contact when they are interested in a conversation. If eyes wander, it might be a polite way of telling you, they'd rather be somewhere else.

Let's talk about their posture. Are they leaning in, showing genuine interest, or are they leaning away or even angling their body towards the door, signaling a desire to escape? Body orientation can speak volumes about a person's level of engagement in a conversation.

Next, what about their arms? Are they crossed defensively, or are arms casually at their sides or engaged in occasional gesturing? While crossed arms don't always signify a defensive stance, in a casual conversation, it might indicate unease or discomfort.

Remember, the legs often reveal what the mind wants to do. A person might do an excellent job of maintaining upper body engagement, but if their feet are pointed away, they likely want to leave the conversation. Foot direction is usually an unconscious act and can be a reliable cue to discern one's true intentions.

The tone and volume of their voice can also provide clues. A softer, lower-pitched voice can indicate boredom, disinterest, or a desire not to be overheard, while a louder and more animated tone could suggest enthusiasm and energetic engagement.

Also, pay attention to any physical barriers they may create, like holding a drink or bag between you two. These subtleties could be seen as an attempt to establish some distance or protect personal space.

Behaviors such as touching their face or tapping their fingers or feet can illustrate impatience or restlessness. However, remember everyone has different habits. Some people might naturally be more fidgety than others without it significantly reflecting their state of mind. It's key to take note of such gestures, but don't directly label them cues of disinterest.

Now, let's look at timing and synchrony. Is the person mirroring your behaviors? Picking up their glass when you do, or answering quickly and fluidly to your comments? Synchrony is usually a good sign of rapport and can mean your time together is going well.

While understanding these signals, remember to consider the context and combine multiple body language signs to form an opinion. Relying on a single cue might lead to misinterpretation.

Finally, keep in mind there's a significant difference between 'noticing' and 'staring'. While reading body language is essential, ensure your efforts aren't getting creepy. It's all about being subtle and maintaining respect towards the other person's personal space.

In conclusion, when you're hearing all the verbal 'yes's but seeing body language 'no's, it's essential to trust your instincts. Body language is a vital key which can unlock the mystery of human intentions, be it with an acquaintance, friend, or loved one. Mastering this art can certainly keep you one step ahead in the conversation traversing the landscape of human interaction with ease and confidence.

Through conscious observation and practice, you can soon become adept at these non-verbal messages. Remember, body language is like another language spoken silently. While the initial stages of learning might seem challenging, over time it can evolve into an intuitive skillset that empowers you to understand others beyond their spoken words.

Chapter 6:
Enhancing Personal Communication

So, you've mastered the nuances of reading body language. That's a great start! But remember, communication is a two-way street. It's not just about understanding others. It's also about how you're being understood. This chapter will take you on a deep dive into body language self-awareness. You'll come to understand your unconscious signals, ensuring you're not sending the wrong message. Just as you can use body language to understand another person's thoughts and intentions, others can, and will, judge you based on your non-verbal behavior. That's why you need to adjust and adapt your body language. If you're interacting with a defensive person, for instance, you might mirror their body language to establish trust and defuse the situation. Don't forget, your body language can be a powerful tool in negotiation, in expressing empathy, or even in diffusing potential conflicts. It's essential, therefore, to master not only the art of reading but also controlling your body language. Let's dig in on how you can communicate more effectively through your own non-verbal cues in this enthralling journey of personal communication.

Body Language Self-Awareness

We've been discussing the world of body language, how it plays a huge role in our interactions with others, and how you can read it to unlock the unspoken emotions and intentions of the people around you. However, recognizing the importance of our own body language is just as vital. This section is all about body language self-awareness, or how you exhibit non-verbal cues and how they impact your interactions with others.

To start off, let's talk about the mirror technique. iMirror technique is about observing yourself in order to understand your non-verbal cues. Sounds simple, right? But it's easier said than done. Have you ever watched yourself on a video and felt uncomfortable with what you saw? Possibly your own gestures, expressions or postures, seemed unfamiliar or odd? This happens because we are often unaware of our own body language.

If you can, record yourself during a typical conversation. Alternatively, in front of a mirror, re-enact previous conversations and try to be aware of your own actions. Pay attention to your facial expressions, posture, hand gestures, and even the way you move. As you evaluate, you'll start noticing trends or behaviors that you may not have been aware of before.

Posture is a significant aspect of your body language. Do you slouch or stand tall? Do you lean in when talking or keep your distance? Your posture conveys a range of signals. Stooping or slouching can send signals of low confidence or lack of interest, while standing tall can convey confidence and engagement.

Next in line are your facial expressions. They are often the most indicative of your emotions and thoughts. Are you someone who can't help smiling when you're happy or frowning when you're upset? Or do you have a poker face? People regularly evaluate others' facial expressions to interpret their state of mind, so being aware of what your face is saying can significantly influence your interactions.

Hand gestures also play a role in how our message is interpreted. Are your hand movements synchronized with your spoken words? Or are they subdued, and if so, is this intentional? You should be mindful of your hand movements because, intentionally or not, they convey significant meaning during conversation.

Proximity, or your personal space, is another facet of body language that's worth mentioning. How close do you stand or sit to someone when you're having a conversation? Do you find personal space so essential that you always maintain a good distance, or are you a close talker? Recognize that although you may be comfortable with a certain proximity, others might not be.

If you've been neglecting your feet, you're missing a vital part of self-aware body language. Your feet often share candid information about your feelings and thoughts. Are they usually pointed towards the door, illustrating your repeated desire to leave? Or do they point towards the person you're talking to, showing your engagement and interest in the conversation?

Your voice tone also contributes to how your message is perceived. Do you speak too softly, or are you naturally loud? How about your pacing or occasional mumbling? Understanding your voice and how it sets the tone of your interactions is critical. In some cases, it might not be what you say, but how you say it that matters most.

Now, as we talk about all this, don't get the impression that there's a universally 'right' or 'wrong' way to use body language. Instead, what's key is understanding that your non-verbal cues can significantly affect how others perceive you. By being more self-aware, you can choose to adjust your body language in ways that will enhance your communication.

Remember, self-awareness is not about identifying flaws. It's about understanding your strengths and weaknesses. We all have tendencies that might not serve us best in every situation. The goal is to become cognizant of them and adapt as required.

One of the best advantages of self-aware body language is that it allows for adaptation. When your actions align with your intentions, others are more likely to trust and understand you. But, if your body language is out of sync with your words, it can create confusion or mistrust.

In sum, body language self-awareness is an underutilized tool that can help you navigate social and professional scenarios more effectively. By being aware of our own non-verbal signals, we can work towards enhancing our interactions to be more compelling, empathetic, and persuasive.

Adjusting and Adapting Your Own Body Language

Body language plays an integral role in how we communicate and interpret those around us. As much as it's crucial to read others' body language, it's equally imperative to understand and adjust our own body language. This awareness and control of our non-verbal cues enhance personal interactions, both professionally and socially.

Your body language is an outward display of your inner state. Hence, it can't be manipulated without affecting your emotional and mental state. You can't simply decide to stand in a confident manner while feeling completely insecure inside. However, certain techniques can be employed to enhance your posture, gestures, and facial expressions, which in turn can influence your overall body language.

Start off by observing your natural body language. Take note of how you sit, stand, or move when you're relaxed or stressed. These observations can shed some light on your personal body language vocabulary, and it can be the basis from which you start modifying your behavior.

Posture is often underestimated, yet it speaks volumes. An upright posture exudes confidence, openness, and alertness, whereas slouching or hunching over can be interpreted as lack of interest, low self-esteem, or even defensiveness. Practicing good posture involves aligning your spine, relaxing your shoulders, and engaging your core muscles. It might feel unnatural initially, but with time, this can have profound effects on your attitude and interactions.

Gestures are also a significant part of your body language. They should be purposeful and fitting to the conversation. However, being overly expressive or using repetitive gestures can detract from your words and cause confusion. One common tip is to avoid crossing your arms. This can be seen as a defensive or closed-off posture. Instead, keep your arms relaxed and use them to punctuate or illustrate your words for more effective communication.

Facial expressions are the most visible aspects of body language. They are often the first thing people notice and therefore carry a significant weight in shaping first impressions. The most impactful way to adjust your facial expressions is to make sure they are synchronized with your words. Congruence between what you say and how you look while saying it strengthens your message.

Maintaining eye contact is a powerful tool in communication. It proves your interest in the conversation and increases the level of engagement. However, too intense or prolonged eye contact can be off-putting. To maintain suitable eye contact, focus on looking at the other person's eyes for a few seconds, then shift your gaze to what they are referring to or slightly to the side. Avoid looking down, as it can suggest timidity or submission.

The way you position yourself in relation to others also plays a key role in communication. Facing someone directly indicates your full attention while turning your body away from another might be interpreted as avoidance or lack of interest. Hence, ensuring your positioning complements your interactions and message can go a long way.

Tone of voice and speech play a part in body language as well. Speak with a steady and confident tone, avoid filler words like "um" or "uh", and use pauses to underscore important points. Remember, your words can hold more weight when delivered effectively with corresponding body language.

Practicing personal space can also improve your body language. Everybody has their own comfort zone when it comes to physical distance. Encroaching upon someone's personal space may come off as aggressive or intrusive. Maintain a comfortable distance during conversations, neither too close nor too far away. This can lead to more enjoyable and effective interactions.

Mirroring, when done subtly, can help build rapport with the other person. It involves reflecting their body language, gestures, or tone in a gentle manner. It creates an unspoken bond and makes the person feel more comfortable and better understood. However, excessive or poorly executed mirroring can make you appear insincere or mocking.

Learning to adjust and adapt your body language won't happen overnight. It's an ongoing process that involves self-awareness and targeted improvements. It's about creating harmony between your external body language and your internal state. With practice, conscious modification becomes an unconscious habit, one that will stand to benefit you in the various domains of life.

It's important to remember that while enhancing your body language can lead to improved personal and professional interactions, it's also about authenticity. Your body language should be a testament to your true feelings and thoughts, not a facemask. It's about finding the balance between displaying approachable and effective body language and being genuine to who you truly are.

By learning to adapt and adjust your own body language, you not only control your narrative but you can also contribute positively to the emotional state of those around you. It's a mightily powerful tool that can help create strong bonds, establish trust, and enrich every personal interaction. Remember, it's not just about analyzing, but also being conscious and purposeful about your own non-verbal communication.

Chapter 7:
Case Studies: Real-Life Applications

In the practical world, recognizing body language cues significantly ups our game in understanding people and predicting their potentially actions. Let's dive straight into some real-world applications by examining political figures. Ever noticed the confident strut of a seasoned politician, or the earnest hand gestures of an impassioned leader? These aren't frivolous details. They're calculated moves designed to garner trust and project authority. Similarly, celebrity interviews offer a goldmine of non-verbal cues. All that laughter, leaning in, or a flitting look of discomfort—it's not just about what they say but also how they say it. And let's not forget everyday scenarios. Remember catching your co-worker's fleeting frown during that meeting, or your friend's eyes lighting up at your suggestion? These micro-expressions and subtle postures contribute volumes to the narrative. It's by digging into these instances using our new understanding of body language that we can derive richer, more insightful interpretations of the dance of communication unfolding around us.

Political Figures

Political figures are prime examples when it comes to the study of body language. Every gesture, tone, and facial expression they use are meticulously designed to influence public opinion, enhance their credibility, or achieve buy-in for their policies. Body language, for these individuals, is more than just unspoken communication; it's a strategic tool. Let's delve into some examples for a more comprehensive understanding.

Take, for instance, power postures. Political figures often engage in power posing to exhibit confidence and authority. Straight backs, chest out, hands either firmly on the sides or confidently gesturing, these are signs of an individual asserting dominance and seeking to command attention. During speeches or debates, you might notice politicians use wide arm gestures. This isn't unintentional. Wide gestures communicate openness, determination, and surety in one's beliefs.

When it comes to eye contact, political figures often use it as a powerful tool. Holding and maintaining eye contact with listeners communicates sincerity, creates a bond with the audience, and fosters a sense of intimacy. Conversely, a politician who frequently breaks eye contact during crucial moments of discourse might be perceived as being deceptive, evasive, or untrustworthy.

Facial expressions are another critical element in the political arena. An effective political figure knows the importance of smiling at the right moments to demonstrate empathy and understanding. Furrowing one's brow, meanwhile, might suggest that the individual is engaged in deep thought or shows concern. Squinting could be interpreted as skepticism, while a nod can suggest agreement or understanding. These non-verbal cues and their interplay weave a tapestry of nuanced communication that goes beyond mere words spoken.

Body positioning matters too. Consider how political figures appear in photographs or on stage. Are they positioned centrally and prominently? This conveys a message of leadership and importance. Are they inclined toward someone? This signifies a connection and rapport with that individual, expressing alliance or favor.

Decoding Silence

The use of touch in body language, especially among political figures, is interesting. Whether it's a handshake, a comforting pat on the back, or a friendly arm around the shoulders, each gesture carries meaning. A weak handshake could be seen as a lack of confidence or determination, while a too strong one might suggest aggression or over-assertiveness. On the other hand, a firm, balanced handshake often communicates respect, rapport, and equality.

Another essential factor to pay attention to unfolds in debates or panel discussions. How candidates engage with one another, react to statements, or even handle interruptions can offer valuable insights into their personalities. It's all about noticing the silent cues - a subtle smirk, a roll of the eyes, the raising of eyebrows, shrugging of shoulders - each of these minute expressions offers a clue into the individual's thought process, emotions, or attitudes towards the topic or the person they're engaging with.

Then there's the voice - a crucial component of a politician's toolset. A warm and confident tone can earn a politician points in the likability factor, and a measured pace can portray them as thoughtful and composed, even under pressure. Rising intonations at the end of their sentences, meanwhile, can imply that they're open to discussing the topic further, while a consistent pace and tone can demonstrate conviction and certainty.

Understanding the body language cues of political figures isn't just about analysis for the sake of it. It's a way for voters to understand who they're putting their trust in, beyond the promises and rhetoric. When words and non-verbal cues align, you know you're dealing with someone sincere. When there's a mismatch, though, it's a cue to dig deeper and question credibility.

It's also worth noting that public figures, especially politicians, receive training in body language. They're schooled in which poses to adopt, gestures to use, expressions to wear and even where to look. They know that their every move is being observed and interpreted.

Not just by body language experts, but by voters whose decisions are influenced by their perceptions of honesty, decisiveness, and sincerity.

Reading and understanding these non-verbal cues in the context of political communication can not only make for a fascinating study but can also leave you more informed and equipped to make confident decisions. Reading beneath the surface, beyond the words and into the silent messages whispered through body language, arms you with a greater understanding of the individuals vying for influence, power, and leadership.

Crucially, reading political figures' body language enhances your ability to discern their true emotions and motives, enabling a more-rounded understanding. If you want to cut through the political spin and see the person behind the politics, body language won't lie. It's a tool, a silent language, that when understood, can reveal more than words ever can.

Before we wrap up this section, it's important to note that despite their training, politicians are merely human. Like all of us, they have ticks, tells and body language habits that are deeply ingrained and unguarded. These moments, when the persona slips slightly, can be the most revealing of all. Keep an eye out for those, because they offer raw glimpses into the individual's true character and personality.

Lastly, remember that body language is rich and complex. Learning to read it successfully, especially in the political context, requires practice and patience, but it's undoubtedly worth it. It adds a layer of understanding that goes beyond verbal communication, deepening your insight not just into the realms of politics, but into the nuances of human communication more broadly.

Celebrity Interviews

The art of body language interpretation is never more publicly on display than during celebrity interviews. These captivating encounters, viewed by millions, provide rich material to the sharp-eyed observer.

So, how can we harness our understanding of body language to decode these high-profile communications? Let's delve in.

Consider the pressure-cooker environment of a live interview. It's packed with tension, combining bright studio lighting, high-stakes questions, and an international audience eagerly awaiting every word. It's within this setting that the body language of these global personalities can reveal their true emotions and intentions, sometimes more than their polished words can.

Scrutinizing body language during celebrity interviews enables us to recognize when a person is genuinely relaxed or just pretending to be. The difference is like night and day. The relaxed interviewee often leans back, maintaining an open stance, possibly even gesturing dynamically during the conversation. On the other hand, when someone is tense, they may lean forward or clench their jaws, and their movements can seem rigid or forced.

For example, an open palm gesture communicates honesty and openness, but it's crucial not to dismiss the context in which this gesture is made. If everything else aligns - relaxed position, pleasant facial expression, natural dialogue - it's a strong sign of authenticity. Conversely, if the gesture is contradicted by other body language elements, then it may signal duplicity.

Eye contact is another crucial aspect to consider. Too much eye contact can be a sign of an overbearing or controlling person, while too little suggests avoidance or lack of confidence. An optimal mix signifies a balanced, engaged participant in conversation, who is neither over-imposing nor evasive. The tell is in the little details, like a fleeting glance away while contemplating an answer, then a shift back to firm, assertive eye contact, balancing politeness with sincerity.

Furthermore, the interviewer themselves, often a celebrity in their own right, gives us a chance to scrutinize their body language. The way they interact with their guests, their control over the narrative, their reactions to answers, all provide clues to their perspectives and emotions.

Facial expressions are another important aspect of body language in interviews. Genuine smiles involve both the zygomatic major muscle (raising the corners of the mouth) and the orbicularis oculi muscles (causing crow's feet around the eyes). Conversely, 'social' smiles involving the mouth only often indicate acting or pretending to be amiable.

Moreover, note how actors handle questions about their co-stars' performances or their feelings about a script. If they express positive sentiments verbally, but their faces reveal thinly masked expressions of boredom or hostility, it's an indication that they're not being entirely honest.

Defensive positions, such as crossed arms or legs, can suggest a person is uncomfortable and closing off from the conversation. Just as revealing is how the individual may adjust their stance upon receiving a challenging question. Do they instantly cross their arms? This might indicate they are now on the defensive. Again, it's essential to take the overall context into account before jumping to conclusions.

Remember, body language interpretation is not about a one-to-one mapping of certain movements or gestures to specific meanings. It's about noticing patterns, nuances, and inconsistencies in the overall context of an interaction. Celebrity interviews, so full of rich non-verbal information, provide a fascinating field for such observation and analysis.

Get ready to watch costumes and glamor fade into the background as you tune into the real life drama played out in the non-verbal communications of the world's most watched personalities. We've told you what to look for - enigmatic smiles, the 'open' palms that might say more than meets the eye, or the sudden straightening of the back. After all, it's these subtle signals that form the truly fascinating buzz behind the spotlight.

By carefully observing and understanding these signals, not only can we get a deeper insight into the minds of our favorite celebrities, but we can also hone our skills in reading and interpreting body language in our everyday interactions. This can pave the way towards improved communication, greater understanding of others, and better relationships in our personal and professional lives.

In conclusion, the skills you've been working on throughout this book find a vivid application in the world of celebrity interviews. By carefully observing and interpreting these encounters, you become an active participant in the art of body language decoding. It's an often subtle, always fascinating linguistic dance, where knowledge truly brings power - the power to see beyond the words and truly understand what's being 'said'.

Everyday Scenarios

The world itself is a classroom, teaching us pertinent lessons about the language of our bodies. Body language is not reserved for special occasions or grand events. It's a daily occurrence, woven into every conversation and interaction we have. In this section, let's explore how the art of reading body language plays out in ordinary, everyday scenarios.

Imagine you're standing in line for your morning coffee. There's a couple in front of you. They're not speaking—it seems far too early for that—but their body language speaks volumes. The woman quietly leans into the man, her body angled towards his. The man, meanwhile, pats her hand softly, his gaze firmly fixed on her. It's a silent scene of affection, revealed not by words but by the language of their bodies. Such every-day moments can be a rich source of understanding about subtle emotional cues.

Consider another scene: you're in a library, huddled in your corner, engrossed in a good book. But something makes you look up, and you spot two people engaged in what appears to be an intense conversation. One's arms are crossed, his stance rigid; the other is leaning back, eyes darting around the room. The defensive posture of the first suggests he's resistant or uncomfortable, the aloofness of the second hints at disinterest or unease. You don't need to hear their conversation to know that it's fraught with tension.

Let's take a trip to the supermarket. Aisles filled with people, each one communicating in their own silent language. There's a man examining a can of soup, his brows furrowed in concentration. A woman hesitates near the dairy section, eyes roaming, hand absently tapping her cart handle. All of these actions reveal their hidden thoughts, offering a glimpse into their decision-making process, if you take the time to read them.

How about an evening at a local park? There's a father sitting on a bench, observing his child play. His legs are crossed, chin resting pleasantly on his hand, a smile playing gently on his face. His comfortable posture suggests relaxation while his focused gaze speaks volumes of his interest in his child's activities.

Even in more intimate settings, like a dinner date, body language plays a starring role. Observe carefully and you might notice the softening eyes of your date, the slight tilt of their head when they're truly listening, or the broadening of their back when they are tucking into their favorite dish. Understanding such exchanges of body language can ensure a smooth conversation and a successful date!

Ever stood at a bus stop observing your co-passengers? Their stance, the way they glance at their watch or the distant road, or the nervously tapping foot—all these are indicators of their state of mind, revealing impatience or relaxation. Body language, when read correctly, can tell you if you should strike up a conversation or offer the person some space.

Even at the end of a tiring day, when you're lounging at home with your family, body language is an active participant in your interactions. A sibling sprawled out comfortably on the couch signals contentment;

a parent's tired but loving gaze reaffirms their affection without the need for any spoken assurances.

What about in situations that require delicate handling, like comforting a friend who's going through a tough time? Their slumped shoulders, downcast eyes, and silent tears are a language of their own, calling for your gentle words and support.

Take a look in the mirror, too. You'll find that you too are unconsciously speaking through your movements and gestures. A victorious fist pump when you reach a milestone, the half-smile playing on your lips recalling a joyful memory, the firm set of your shoulders before a challenging task—all of these reveal your inner thoughts and emotions.

We often neglect these everyday scenarios, failing to realize their instructive potential. But once you appreciate and understand body language, you'll see them as a treasure trove of knowledge. Use them to practice and hone your skills, because every interaction is a chance to learn a little more about the human spirit.

To master the art of deciphering body language, you don't always need grand stages or dramatic events. Sometimes, all it takes is a simple cup of coffee, a quiet library corner, or a leisurely stroll in the park. The world, in all its everyday ordinariness, is a ripe ground for learning, if only you find the time to pause, observe, and understand.

These everyday scenarios are the most practical demonstrations of the knowledge you've gathered about body language, and they are also the most consistent practice fields. Everyday scenarios push us to shift our learning from theoretical constructs to practical implementations, thereby enhancing our understanding in the process. So, let's embrace these inimitable lessons that every day brings forth and learn to decipher the silent language that accompanies and elucidates all human interaction.

Remember, life, with all its interactions and exchanges, offers boundless opportunities to understand and interpret body language.

So, don't sideline these moments; rather, use them as a platform to nurture your observational skills, enhancing your understanding of body language and, ultimately, of people.

Chapter 8:
The Impact of Mastering Body Language

As we've delved deeper into the world of body language, it's become quite clear that the mastery of this silently persuasive language can vastly impact both our personal relationships and professional interactions. It's like acquiring an advanced skill set that gives you an irrefutable advantage in the grand dance of human connection, akin to being fluent in a foreign language amidst a sea of non-speakers. You suddenly become adept at anticipating and predicting behavior—an ability that remains elusive to the majority. With this proficiency, you can navigate the complex web of human emotions with an ease that others can only dream of. Personal relationships significantly improve as you're now more in tune with people's emotional states, enabling deeper empathy and understanding. In the workplace, this heightened comprehension bolsters your interactions, helping you build credibility, exhibit leadership, and foster stronger professional bonds. It's like understanding the undertones in a conversation, the invisible thread interweaving the visible ones. This newfound competence in deciphering body language can lift you head and shoulders above the rest in any given situation, cementing your role as a respected pillar in your personal and professional circles.

Advantages in Personal Relationships

Mastering body language can significantly enhance your personal relationships. Just like in a symphony, the music of body language, when understood correctly, can be harmonious and a representation of synchronicity. Let's dig into why this is essential and how it enriches your personal relationships.

When you understand body language trickles, you pay better attention to the unspoken cues your friends, family, or partner are sending your way. The subtleties in their expressions and postures can reveal what they may feel deep down but aren't ready to say out loud. You can sense hesitations, unexpressed longings, discontentment, and even lies like a seasoned detective. This uncanny ability of yours will make you a better listener and, subsequently, a better friend, sibling, or partner.

Body language mastery can also help you act more empathetically. Awareness of people's nonverbal signals enables you to respond to their emotional states more sensitively. For example, if a person appears uncomfortable at a party, you could help alleviate their discomfort by engaging them in conversation or introducing them to others.

A keen understanding of body language can help couples communicate more effectively. A darting eye, a masked smile, or a slump in their shoulders can tell you more about your partner's emotions than a rehearsed 'everything's fine.' You'll know when to provide reassurance, when to give space, or simply when to hold their hand to convey your support.

Conflicts are inevitable in personal relationships. At times like these, body language is a potent weapon to defuse tension. An understanding smile, a gentle touch, or maintaining open postures can help break down barriers and make peace talks easier.

Mastering body language plays a huge role in creating first impressions. Whether it's meeting your partner's parents, striking up a conversation with a stranger or making a new friend, the way you poise yourself nonverbally could either draw them towards you or set them off.

Body language isn't only important in person, but also applies to digital communication. Facial expressions during video calls give away as much information as they do in a face-to-face interaction. So, brushing up on your body language decoding skills can prove advantageous in this tech-fueled era as well.

Getting a hang of body language can turn the tables around for you if you're socially anxious. By understanding others' body language, you can modify your behavior or responses to make the interaction more pleasant. Gradually, this skill can help you navigate social situations with more confidence and ease.

Apart from understanding others' body language, learning to control your own can make you more persuasive and charismatic. You can learn to project confidence, openness, and trustworthiness that would magnetically draw people towards you.

Knowing body language can also act as a reality check. By observing others around you, you can understand if someone is pretending to like you when they don't or understand the real motive behind a person's actions. This can help protect you from negative influences.

Body language is a powerful parenting tool. By understanding their child's nonverbal cues, parents can form a deeper bond. It also helps to identify signs of distress, discomfort, or anticipation, which the child might not be able to express verbally.

A mastery of body language can also help you connect with people who are non-native to your language. This skill will help you convey your emotions and understand others' feelings beyond verbal interactions, thereby breaking down language barriers.

Last but not least, mastering body language enables you to be more self-aware, helping you understand your weaknesses and biases and allowing you to act consciously in reactions and responses during conversations.

As you can see, understanding body language has a significant positive impact on personal relationships. By becoming an adept non-verbal communicator, you stand a better chance of deepening your connections, enhancing empathy, fostering understanding, and navigating social situations efficiently.

This journey towards understanding and mastering body language might seem demanding, but it's worth every effort. After all, being able to connect with others at a deeper level makes our relationships more rewarding and life more meaningful.

Improved Professional Interactions

Harnessing the power of body language not only elevates your personal relationships but can markedly improve professional interactions as well. When harnessed and properly interpreted, body language can be integral in understanding how your colleagues and bosses perceive you, and likewise, how you perceive them. It can help in strengthening business relationships, facilitating productive meetings and making presentations resonant and effective.

The first step toward mastering this in a professional setting is building self-awareness. It's all about understanding how your non-verbal cues reflect on others and being cautious about the messages your body might be inadvertently sending. A conscious stance, a controlled tone, and thoughtful facial expressions can make a world of difference. It communicates respect, understanding, and professionalism, setting up a positive atmosphere for the interaction.

It's not uncommon for misunderstandings to occur in the workplace due to miscommunication. These issues most often stem from misreading or completely overlooking non-verbal cues. And make no mistake, even the smallest slips can lead to a domino effect impacting the overall workplace environment. Therefore, reading body language accurately can nip potential conflict in the bud, enhance team cohesion, and create a productive work atmosphere.

Now, look at meetings. They are the crucible where decisions get made, ideas get planted, and professional fates are often decided. These sessions are usually high-stake and teeming with non-verbal exchanges. Being able to read these silent messages gives you a significant edge, providing insights into the intentions and true feelings of your colleagues. A shift in seating position, a discomforting smile, or an authoritative gesture can provide you with a wealth of information, well beyond spoken words.

Similarly, body language mastery gives you an advantage during presentations. This isn't just about reading your audience but also about managing your non-verbal cues to increase your perceived credibility. Powerful presentations are built on clear, impactful speech complimented by strong and confident body language. Proper stance, controlled hand gestures, and engaging facial expressions can make your presentation more persuasive.

Understanding body language can even tip professional negotiations in your favor. Whether it's about salary negotiations, client acquisitions, project management, or dealing with suppliers, mastering body language can give you the edge. Taking calculated steps using insights gathered from non-verbal cues can put you in a strong position. Identifying a sense of unease, a sign of confidence, or a display of transparency can guide you on when to push harder, when to hold back, and when to close deals.

And let's not forget professional networking. Reading body language accurately during networking events can turn serendipitous interactions into fruitful professional relationships. It can give you a good idea of who is approachable, who seems interested in your ideas, and even what topics to steer clear of during conversations. Combined with genuine interest in others, skillful use of body language can set a solid foundation for your professional network.

Professional interactions aren't just confined to the office or traditional workplace either. In this age of digital technology, many such communications occur online. Mastering body language provides techniques to make these virtual interactions just as effective and nuanced as in-person dialogues. The importance of posture, maintaining proper eye contact, and making sure your facial expressions are visible are essential during virtual meetings.

Moreover, training yourself to read body language correctly plays an invaluable role in leadership positions. Leaders who can accurately interpret their team's non-verbal communication cues can create a more engaged and collaborative environment. Recognizing an employee's unspoken concerns or identifying latent team dynamics can help assess situations more effectively and lead to proactive solutions.

Another invaluable aspect of mastering body language in the professional sphere comes during job interviews. Interviewers look at non-verbal cues as much as the answers you provide. And as a prospective employee, understanding the interviewer's body language provides an undercurrent of understanding that can shape your responses. It enhances your chances of making a positive impression and landing the job you want.

Beyond the interviewing process, as a manager, understanding body language can allow you to break down barriers with staff, assisting you in determining what motivates your team, what concerns they have, and ultimately making you a better leader. One who is not only heard but understood.

Promoting this body language awareness and interpreting skills amongst your team can also foster a more transparent and empathic work environment. When each person in the team recognizes the importance of non-verbal communication and strives to understand and be understood, it breeds a positive culture that encourages open communication.

In conclusion, the impacts of mastering body language on professional interactions are far-reaching and profoundly transformative. It's a tool that adds depth to your professional relationships, enhances your leadership prowess, and gives you an unspoken advantage in various professional situations, ultimately boosting your career trajectory.

So we've walked through how enhanced understanding and use of body language can significantly benefit both personal relationships and professional interactions. Up next, we'll delve into how these skills can be further utilized in anticipating and predicting behavior, providing you with that enigmatic ability to stay a step ahead. Stay tuned!

Anticipating and Predicting Behavior

When you've developed an understanding of body language, you can start to use this knowledge to predict and anticipate the behavior of others. It's like having a secret superpower, a decoded window into the unspoken dynamics of human interaction.

Imagine the numerous scenarios where reading body language can give you the upper hand. You meet a new business client for the first time, and the way they stand, their facial expressions, and hand gestures give you a layer of insight into their expectations or their mood. Perhaps you're attending a social event, and you manage to pick up signs that someone is interested in you before they even utter a word. Being able to anticipate and predict behavior through body language allows you to navigate these complex social situations with confidence and ease.

But before we get too excited about our newfound superpower, let's remember that this is not about manipulation or control. It's about understanding others and fostering genuine, mutually beneficial interactions. It's about empathy, respect, and forging stronger connections. Now, without further delay, let's explore how we can apply our understanding of body language to anticipate and predict behavior.

First and foremost, remember that it's essential to take a holistic approach. Body language isn't about isolated gestures or expressions. It's a symphony of signs that work in unison. Don't jump to conclusions based on one single element - context is key. Interpreting body language must always consider the environment, the interaction, and the particular personality of the people involved.

Next, focus on consistency. If someone's verbal and non-verbal signals align, their message is likely to be authentic. However, if their body language is contradicting their words, there might be more to their story.

They may feel uneasy, be withholding information, or possibly even lying. These discrepancies can help anticipate someone's actual feelings or intentions.

Thirdly, look for clusters of signals. When multiple body language signs point in the same direction, it increases the likelihood of accurately predicting behavior. For instance, crossed arms might indicate discomfort, but when combined with a frown and looking away, it's a fair bet that the person is upset or frustrated.

Fourthly, understand that cultural influences and personal habits can affect body language interpretation. What may be seen as a sign of respect in one culture may convey a totally different message in another. Similarly, personal habits or idiosyncrasies may confound standard body language interpretations. Being aware of these nuances can provide more accurate predictions about people's behavior.

Fifthly, remember the role of individual emotion and stress levels. People under stress or experiencing strong emotions are more likely to leak non-verbal cues. By paying close attention to these indicators, you can anticipate reactions and manage your own responses accordingly.

Additionally, recognize the importance of timing. Timing can be critical in interpreting body language and predicting behavior. If a person suddenly changes their posture or expression in response to something said or done, it can be highly revealing about their feelings or thoughts.

One more thing to consider is that body language is dynamic, and people continually adjust their signals based on situations and reactions from others. Mastering body language will allow you to adapt to these changes and maintain an upper hand in conversations and negotiations.

Lastly, be patient. Proficiency in reading body language takes time, experience, and careful observation. The more you practice, the better you'll become at anticipating and predicting behavior. Soon you'll notice that you're not just understanding others better, but you're also more in tune with your own body language and how it impacts your interactions.

In conclusion, the ability to anticipate and predict behavior using body language is a powerful tool in your interpersonal communication kit. It allows you to tailor your interactions dynamically, steer them productively, and build more fruitful relationships both in your personal life and professional sphere.

Remember, this isn't about manipulation or gaining an unfair advantage over others. Instead, it's about fostering mutual understanding and empathy, bridging the gap between what is said and what is felt, and ultimately, creating more harmonious and productive connections with the people in our lives.

Conclusion

As we journey through life, non-verbal communications play a crucial role in our interactions with others. They determine not just the tone and direction of our conversations, but also the nature of our relationships. Grasping the complexities of expressions, gestures, hormonal responses and neurological signs enables us to better understand the motives and emotions of others. This book has aimed to shed light on the different aspects of body language, helping you to become more adept at predicting others' actions and intentions.

The application of body language extends far beyond mere social interactions. Decoding body language can offer a significant edge in professional environments, as you're able to decipher unspoken sentiments and unseen emotions during meetings or presentations. Emotional states, such as happiness, sadness, and anger, often manifested subtly, hold the key to understanding our interlocutor's feelings and points of view. Recognizing these states aids us in tailoring our approach and responses accordingly.

Predicting intentions are of particular importance when it comes to security and safety or when deciphering other core emotions, such as interest and desire. The smallest twitch or the widest smile can provide critical insights into a person's mentality and mindset, allowing you to either prevent unwanted outcomes or foster positive results effectively. Navigating these intricate channels of body language has the power to transform casual conversations into meaningful connections.

Becoming aware of your own body language and its impact on others cannot be overstressed. Any pause, movement, or expression can affect the perception others have of you, consciously or otherwise. Hence, learning to adjust and adapt our body language enables us to create desired impressions and control the narrative to some extent. It's an empowering tool, one that can enhance our personal and professional lives significantly.

Through real-life applications, we understand how body language affects our decisions as a society. The way our leaders speak, their stance, and their facial expressions can influence our perceptions and, ultimately, our choices. By mastering the art of body language, we can better anticipate behavior, navigate social situations, and enrich our relationships. The silent dance of gestures, expressions, and postures might be complex, but with understanding and practice, we can all learn to move to its rhythm.

Appendix A:
Further Resources

Having reached the end of this insightful journey into the world of body language, you're probably keen to keep learning. Below, you'll find a collection of recommended resources to build on the foundation laid out in the previous chapters. It's a mix of books, websites, online courses, and articles that'll help you heighten your understanding and further fine-tune your skills. Practice is key, so why limit yourself?

Books

Here are some recommendations that can help enhance your understanding:

"The Definitive Book of Body Language" by Barbara Pease and Allan Pease: A comprehensive guide that'll help you explore the nonverbal language scope.

"Emotions Revealed" by Paul Ekman: A deep dive into recognizing emotions and understanding people better.

"Everybody is saying it" by Joe Navarro: Provides insight into non-verbal cues which can be used to interpret others' feelings and intentions.

Online Courses

By building on your knowledge through online courses, you can attain a more rounded understanding.

Coursera: Nonverbal Communication - This course offers a banking of lectures and quizzes to test and cement your knowledge.

Udemy: Body Language for Entrepreneurs - It's made for business leaders but truth be told, anyone can benefit from it.

EdX: Becoming An Effective Leader - It includes a module on body language, which can be overlooked but dramatically impactful in leadership roles.

Websites and Articles

These resources give brief, on-the-fly knowledge when you need it:

Psychology Today: A treasure trove of articles about nonverbal communication and interpreting body language.

Body Language Project: This site has information about almost every possible body language cue with illustrative pictures.

Podcasts

For those who prefer to listen and learn, these podcasts are worth seeking out:

The Science of Success: Features guest experts who share insights on various aspects of nonverbal communication.

The Art of Charm: Provides advice and tips on improving social skills, which naturally includes understanding and using body language.

Remember, not everything resonates the same way with everyone. So pick the resources that you think will offer the most value to you. Try mixing and matching books, podcasts, courses, and articles for a more balanced approach to your learning journey. With dedication and practice, you'll continue to improve your body language reading skills and stay ahead in your conversations, relationships, and negotiations.